I Still Believe In Some Things

Anushka Sriram

Dedication

To Aria and Ananya, who are the best parts of me, I am made complete only by the warmth of your friendship

Preface

I've been writing poetry since I was in elementary school, which might make it surprising that I never set out to write a poetry book. These poems started out as bursts of emotion, only communicable through haphazard writing and only understandable to me. Initially, they were all deeply personal recounts of events and emotions I had been through, but somewhere along the way, I discovered that the wonderful thing about being a writer is that you can write about literally anything. You can write pages and pages about what you've never experienced but still somehow feel it—so that's what I did.

This collection is so meaningful to me—and hopefully, it might be to you as well. It's my feelings laid out in words; every time I've loved, grieved, or felt anything too deeply, it's here. Maybe you'll see a reflection of yourself in these pages, or maybe you'll find words for something you couldn't quite name before. Whatever brought you here, I hope you find something that speaks to you. And if you do, then these words have done their job.

Acknowledgements

First and foremost, these poems wouldn't exist without the wonderful people in my life who have supported me at every turn and shaped me into who I am.

To Aria and Ananya—you are the reason these words exist. Thank you for being my constants, for reading every little draft I write, and for standing by my side through it all. I love you immeasurably, and I am immensely grateful to have experienced your companionship. These poems carry pieces of you, and you'll know where to find them.

To my family—thank you for your unwavering dedication to giving me every opportunity in life.

Lastly, an acknowledgment to all the people in my life and the ones no longer in it. These poems are a collection of feelings and a reflection of me, but they are also a collection of you. Every person, every memory, and every emotion that has left an impact on me is woven between the lines of these pages.

This book is as much yours as it is mine.

1. genesis

I had the same dream again – the one woven by you.
                    At night I unravel your silvery
tapestry, and slowly sink myself into it, head first. Where
we wake up with sand in our lungs, the ocean crashing
into our ears, and our hands
                    almost touching.

Tell me again, tell me about the time we
boarded the train to heaven, when our young heartbeats
shook with the thrashing of the engine.

I have always wanted the same things,
I have always wanted you.

When we fell asleep on the altar of the church and I saw
                devotion in a different way than how I
saw it at 14.

Things don't have to end just because they're beautiful.
This feeling is going to be forever.

We were lying in the wet grass behind your sister's
house / the sky full of glittering stars.
                I wanted to swallow them

all, give you something to believe in, to live for. I
remember the coal fire of winter,
 how we thought burning everything meant being free.

The cracks of light poured from me, and when I looked
at you
                                        I knew you
understood, you were the only one to know me.

We sat on the windowsill smoking, and we kept thinking
the world was going to end.

Look at the light fading out, look at the way your heart
starts glowing from the inside.

                I have never got what I wanted.

                Except this, except *you.*

2. passenger seat desire

There's something in the corner of this room. It's
glowing a flushed pink, this white pink aura.
 It walks around my room, all in fluid movements like
water.

                                                 I can't look
it in the eye, if it even has one. Only when it touches me
do I see its hands.

They're my hands.
Same ridges, same scars from
                              being fifteen.

It lies next to me, hand over my chest, right where my
heart beats.

There's somewhere we want to go, and there's two bikes
we can use. I've told you I don't know how to ride a bike,
so we're going on yours.   I can't put my hands
around your waist,
                                          so I'll
be taking my chances with getting hurt.
The last time we were this close I started crying.

I can feel god, but if I reached out to touch him, I'd have

no one but my own pain. It's the same with you. Since I've met you, it's been the end of the world *over and over again.*

We should leave, so we can make these dreams of clean teeth a reality. We should hide in the cargo section of the train and let the light of a new life dawn on us through the windowpane.

Listen to it, this electricity fizzing through our bodies, translating into

I want more, I want more, I want.
I don't know if I have anything to live for other than
the blood rush in my ears and my heart bursting out of my skin.

But now I'm willing to die for it. And that's enough for me.

3. the end times

Blue light cascading your body
And roughened knuckles under my palm
Present tense I want to consume you whole
If it's greed or jealousy
Every breath makes your heart swell ; ripening fruit
This is what it means to want you
And not be wanted back

The phone doesn't work at the gas station anymore
Teenagers in orange light twelve miles from home
I'm scared and I don't want you to see it
Weakness means want / want means shame
You kick the wheel and scream
I put my head on your shoulder
There's a girl you'd bleed for
But all she wants to do is talk on the phone

Beautiful warm sunlight and green plants
White smiles and a record player
Hands on waists and badly cut out red hearts
An image of happiness in pool water
The summer I met you ; when you remember the colours
in your body have a name
This beautiful girl, this beautiful home, wonderful

daydream
In those days I loved to bleed
And you loved to bite

You're sitting behind a girl
Kicks on the shin, muffled giggles
Now everyone's looking at you funny and you're
Romeo with the scrawly handwriting
With a soft promise of forever
Well as long as we both still have blood and teeth, why
not?

Creaks in floorboards
A voice that's supposed to be comforting
Dead winter and the snow crawls up my spine
This is what I think about when you're not there
Humming in the kitchen
I don't think it could hurt any more
Seven years old in a cabin
Happiness is simple and attainable
The pain is raw and fresh all the time
I'm staring out of the window
snow to leaves to sun to rain
I don't want to do this without you

There's someone in your room
Long hair red heels is clearing the bed

The mess would be embarrassing (if you were trying to
impress her)
You hear heels drop to the floor
Slack jaw
You close your eyes and feel the whipping of air when
someone's driving full speed
Spilling energy drinks and walking on the court
Phone smashed on the ground
Warm arms after a fight
Want me want me want me want me
And it's back to the car again
The whole street was flooded
This time I made you bleed
I told you I felt guilty but that wasn't the truth
I wanted to push you over in the water
Taste blood and salt on your lips
Hold your head under till you float / into me

She's already headed to the door by the time your eyes
open
Fizzing numbness sweaty palms a flush face
You're in the shower scrubbing dirt off
Except it's not dirt now it's blood
Except it's not blood now it's her
You want to hear the clack of red heels again so you can
Dream about her again
Pretend once more

This desire is hers

Your hands reach for the dial but
This stupid girl never wants to bite
And I collapse against the wall and weep

Bright fluorescent lighting and bitter coffee
It's next November and i'm starting to think grief is a pit
I have to build my life around
Warm sunshine and laughter and cracks of twigs in
winter
I suppose it means something in the end that I survived
It must have.

4. iscariot's hymn

I watch them take him away, chains locking his wrists.
They're all staring at me in disgust, but the only one I'm
looking at is him.
He knows what I've done, and he knows what's going to
happen to him.

I look into his eyes. He loves me. Still.
It's so true, it's so perfect I want to laugh.
Son of god, our messiah, my saviour.

My kiss has doomed you / you have doomed me with
your love
I will never remember anybody else
Surely you know what waits for your apostle

I loved you the way all humanity has loved – with
violence
You loved me how all gods have – in ways I don't
understand

Damned, I am abhorred
A wretched slave who sold my friend for thirty pieces of
silver
I am the greed and selfishness inherent in every human

Look, they scream. How the bastard's betrayal is met
with forgiveness. They forget.
You are still Jesus Christ. I am still Judas Iscariot.
This story never changes.

I am loved
But I am a sinner
And for that I will pay

5. a story that did not happen

In a story that did not happen
We met and exchanged keys
And we ate month old takeout from your fridge.
I think your roommate hates me.

You caught my jacket down the yogurt aisle
                    And I did not know what to do
with your laugh except for breathe it in
              my oxygen

In words that never existed
          We raced on Brooklyn Bridge, you told me
your father died
Morbidly curious and stupidly insensitive I asked
              Drunk car crash.
                        It does not matter. It
does not matter. It does not matter.
Do you want ice cream?

          Even in a tale stitched from imagination

  Do you like seeing me like this?

I cried when you left my room.
            Only to come back with certain advances -
and prowess
Funny way of eating bones. Leave nothing behind that's
what your dad told you
I'm sorry. Nevermind.

  You cut your people like you cut yourself. The mess of
red string and fuzz.   I like your unraveling tapestry.

I like your way of loving, none at
all.   You said that's what happens when
your parents screwed up.   A wounded child wants
another gash to forget the last one.

In this fabricated story that never happened.
I hate your mom.
            I hate your cigarettes.
                    I want to say I hate you
But you are sleeping. It's terrifying. I'm trying not to
look glassy eyed but you're breathing so slowly I can't
look away,   I need your chest
to rise again.

I slowly climb onto you
      Very still

You're very quiet

I hate you
I spit in your face

Do you still love me? You whispered on the curb.
Fuck you. And your raspy shitty smoker voice.
I did not mention, I did not say
*I cannot stop. Your voice gives me no words to write. I
have nothing to say. How do I tell them that the painters
must've stopped painting and the writers stopped
writing and god stopped creating because you are larger
than language and you are larger than what we can
perceive you are.*

You simply, you are.

I throw up and I throw up and I

lay my guts onto pavement but I fear
you have seeped in my skin like venom.

You are letters and words and sentences stringed
together and this never happened but
Few days before you told me you couldn't say it

You can't say you love me

your dad's genes
                              I guess he gave you something else
too.

I would've taken you any way you came. Even dead.

You were always trying to say things with too much of it
stuck in the back of your throat. I still wonder about all
the conversations that never made it. If *I love you* was in
any of them.

It's all in your subconscious you know, all the shit that
happens in life. It's still there, you don't see it
                              Your voice on
the phone, hours before.

In this story that never happened
                              Because it didn't
                              Because you're
not dead and your car isn't in a junkyard
Because you're not real
I still wait for you to take your keys back.

6. dream of you

In my dream I saw a shadow figure treading lightly
behind me.
            It didn't feel malicious, it was just there.

It gave me purple eyebags and a large satchel with
nothing to put in it. My hands have been heavy since
birth.   I wanted to twist it off

            and put it there so it wouldn't feel so
heavy. The bag I mean, I was always going to feel the
weight of my hands.

In my dream I saw him first, and then I saw you.   And
once I did he started disappearing, face, feet and all.
I ran to the horse stables and found a dictator there.
I don't smoke but we blew puffy rings in the
air   and I asked him what did he want.
                              He said he wanted to
smoke some more,   so we did.
I never knew what you wanted.
            At some point I thought it was me,
but that was stupid, naive.

            You couldn't even want yourself.

Suppose nobody does.
We all want to
disappear like he did when I saw you, face, feet and all.
It's so funny, because at some point we all *do* disappear.

The first time I didn't want to was when we were
walking in a park.

Not a dream. Held your hand.

Everything is painful
without you.

My hands are always wondering why the spaces and
groves are empty.
Nothing belongs to me anymore.   That
happens, when your body was someone else's. It's thrust
back to you again
and you don't know what to do with
it.   You never did,
that's why you were
always looking for somebody else to take it.

When I close my eyes and dream, I dream of you.
And what I don't want to admit is, when I close my eyes
and dream,

I dream of somebody who makes it all light.

Someone
who tells me who I'm supposed to be.
The shadow figure sits behind
me.   I think it's sad, always at a distance.
It never speaks, but I can feel anguish pouring out
of it, and I can feel all the shame

that comes with wanting to be wanted too.

In my dream I laid on the concrete and wondered where
to go after losing your best friend.

Everything about you is past tense, except for love.
And I would tell you about this dream, but we don't
talk.
Except in parts of my brains exchanging neurons.

I want to tell you about this dream, without telling it to
you, without you in it.
I want to sleep without torment,   I want
to forget you calling me your home.

You did
want to run away from home a lot.

In the dream I talk to you. But you only talk about
him.

You're talking and you're talking and it's October
again.   You suddenly hold my hand.
                              You say you're sorry. I
didn't deserve it. You loved - sorry love me, present
tense. You're sorry. It's all in my throat.

*Come back. I don't want him, I want you. If you come
back I'll leave him. Proper, forever. Let's try again, let's
try one last time. Let me love you close-by, then shoot
me. Let me bleed out without me begging for it. I love
you, I love you. I don't want to die, except that I really
want to. But at least I can pretend I don't, in front of you.
For you. Please.*

I'm about to vomit.
    I'm going to say it.
         I'm going to kill myself.
                    I wake up before any of those
things.

the head crumples into my hands, because it's the only
place I know where to put it nowadays.
I wake up with dreams of apologies and dreams of being
light again.   Dreams of you.

7. frankenstein

I'm on my way home and blood is gushing in my
mouth.
     I think my nose is cracked but that's a
blur at the back of my mind.
 I go home / home and I die on the front doorstep.

No, you die on the doorstep. But you already died, before
I came home.
   Oh, I killed you.
     It's your blood.
 You put up a good fight, my broken nose. Dinner,
on the counter. It's ready.
 Who made dinner?
     It's pasta. You always did like
it. Too crimson, strange meat.
The water cooler's bubbling.
  Let it flood the house.
    I'll drown, I'll pull god down with me.
For all the times there wasn't quite enough air in my
lungs, I will drown god with me.

    I'll bring my mother too. They're the
same   Mothers and gods.

Giving birth to a creation they wanted to be, cowards,
both of them.

I'm digging out dirt with my nails.
            The last time you painted my nails.   Hot pink
makes me look garish.

You were a horrible friend.
 I loved you.

So what, so what.
                We kill the things we love, we do not
deserve happiness.

        We would rather tear apart what we love

                        then accept this anomaly.
You're standing over me,
your hand glides down my shoulder and
squeezes.   Did I ever tell you I stole your clip? I
hope you die.
                Actually I killed you so the problem is solved.
Your body looks odd, all muddled and soiled.
                                                My
nails dig into your flesh, we're embracing now.

I wish someone would pour the dirt on me, I don't want

to die but I deserve it.

                        I always want what I do not
deserve, what I have no right to have

                              Your body's covered.
The mess is over.

Your hand curls down further,

             It seems almost
reassuring.   I close my eyes in pain, I've
given you

    the one thing in death I cannot obtain - peace.

The bed is warm, it could just be the blood pooling round
the sheets.

You've been dead a long time.

I'm not sorry about what I did.   Sorry
you trusted a monster,

    and maybe sorry I believed a miscreant could've
been good, could've loved, could've been

               human.

I wake up and go to your house.

          You're still there, I'm not surprised.

                  We talk about what to

get for dinner.
You tell me you love me. I pity you.

There
is no god, I say softly, there are no saviours.
There's no angel of light inside all of us.

It's humans,
and - it's me.   You scream at me but nothing
changes.   I can feel you waning, fading in and out of
existence.

If I could, I'd give this beating pulsating heart to you.
I'd cradle your love and
we can pretend you loved someone good. To not change
is the cruelest – and the most painful.   I want to be
good, I cry out.
Please! Someone hear me!
I want to be good! I want to be worthy!
Please make me
human!   But I knew god was for the good ones,
those without the darkness in them,
The chosen ones.   I could break my fist
banging the door, but no one was going to let me in.

You keep telling me you love me.
I am only saddened by your fate,   some poor
angel missed out on your love because here I was,
lapping it up,   too afraid to want for

more. Too brave to shrink away.

I go out to buy cigarettes.   When I
return you are not there.

             I beg a merciful being to take me away,

What mercy exists for the sinful?

        In Satan's deepest dreams, he wonders why god
did not make him worthy of salvation.

I close my eyes as tight as I can and

                                    trudge back to
your burrow of dirt.

I feel the cold creep up my body, pressing hard against
my ribs.

                              I wish I was
good, but it remains what it always was, a wish.

8. oranges and pomegranates

December 16th. You took two oranges from the kitchen. I took a pomegranate because I didn't want to look useless. Your nimble fingers pried apart the skin, forming two large, curved orange-skin bowls. Deftly, you split the fruit in two and began removing the bitter, flimsy white cover. I watched as you dug nails—nails that took you seven months to grow—into the fleshy pulp to wrench away the seeds. Holding the slice from its open top end, you pulled apart its transparent layer and left the fat, sticky tangelo for me to eat. You did this so carefully—for seventeen slices. Each took you forty-six seconds. Fifty-two if it was smaller because it was harder not to mess up.

I want you to look at me. Really look at me. See who I am. I think you don't, which is why you love me. Sometimes, when you're sitting on the counter, I think to myself: *You don't know the monstrosity that resides in me. You don't know at all.*

I have to get a knife for the pomegranate. This is the first difference. I cannot pry open a pomegranate with my choppy fingernails or the brute strength of my knuckles. When I cut, I always destroy a few seeds, and the red tint splashes onto my sleeves and the wooden board. I

wrench away the skin, dragging the blade to where it
refuses to let go. I end up with a misshapen, deformed
fruit. I try not to audibly make a noise of
disappointment. I skim the membrane off with the blunt
end of the knife.
I start picking up the seeds and putting them in a bowl.
My nails pierce through them, and it makes me so sad to
be giving you this. Red juice runs down my wrists. I'm
ashamed. It takes me four seconds to pull out a seed.
There are three hundred twenty-four seeds in it.
Trembling, I offer you my mutilated, bruised
pomegranate. I feel so silly.
You give me beautiful oranges, and I give you all I have.
And all I have is ugliness and misery & years of being
unlovable.
I'm sorry this is all I turned out to be. I'm sorry I took up
this space on your chair that was clearly somebody
else's. That I growled and snapped and tore it from
somebody else's teeth. I regret like a dog after biting.

9. this is how I know

That it was real.

I would like to — sprawl face down in the dirt so I can't fall anymore. Smell the petrichor and rain instead of your hair. Circling around each other, the snake that's eating its own tail. I'm standing on the same ground where the massacre happened, when I bled out in any way that mattered. I'm the only proof it even happened. I didn't know I was capable of such love, I'm still grieving today – that's how I know. I dreamt I twisted myself over into an alternate dimension, where you were in my rear view instead of glimpses in trees, and strangers, and texts. I'm not laying myself in a grave, but just for a minute I want the dirt to cover my ears. The only time I have prayed is when I have called out your name. I always knew my dreams were foolish, but in dead winter fire is fire, and god this longing is killing me.

Sometimes, they call your name and I look up, it's as good as my own.

10. on mothers

a mother is a very special thing, a very unique thing.
    every part of you is made from your mother. you
may believe god has given you life, an existence.
yet it's your mother who makes it all.

the only difference between a god and a mother is that
you witness a mother's injustice.

you are your mother before you are yourself.

    and she will never let you forget that.
        a mother and daughter have very different
perceptions of each other.

what they rarely know is this perception is not unique,
nothing original.

you want an apology from your mother.
your mother wants an apology from her mother.
and she wants an apology from her mother.
  and she wants an apology from her mother
      and she wants an apology from her mother
          and she wants an apology from her mother.

all you want are apologies,   and all you get are fists
and a mixture of blood and bile

                                in your throat.

say you're sorry for doing this to me.
                                        I never got
mine, why should you?
 tell me why you made me like this.
                                If I knew the answer,
would it change anything? you are still you.
can you fix me? can you make me whole?
                                        ask god.

YOU ARE MY GOD. YOU ARE MY CREATOR.

   I am your mother.
what's the difference?
                        (bitterly) god did not have to cut
pieces of him to create.
        he could make something out of nothing.
mothers create from themselves.
your flesh, your bones, your eyes, everything was
mine.   my future, who I could have been is you now.
I am not you.
                so you believe. and so did I once.

and what about fathers?
what about the men who float around the house?
it takes you twenty years to realize he abandoned you
before you were even born.

 he doesn't speak when he doesn't want to.   you can
scream in his face all you like, it takes you twenty years
to realize you've been living with a ghost.

        when he is angry it shakes the whole house.
whether you like it or not your eyes well with
tears.   you feel your heart decay. it's a betrayal of
sorts.   *you were supposed to be the one I could*
depend on.

you grow up your whole life comparing your mom and
dad,
        deciding who is worse and who is
better,   who was the victim

and who was the killer.

until you finally know you've been living in a house of
killers.
and if you think you're the victim, you're not.

my mother's anger is
a crack of thunder.
 it whips across you, fast and distorting and
painful.   the indentation in your skin will disappear,
             but never from your blood.   your
mother's anger rests in your veins. her sadness fossilizes
into your hatred.

I've spent my whole life trying not to be my creator.
but what choice do daughters have, except to leave like
their fathers,

         and scream like their mothers. what's the
difference between holding a hand and gouging the flesh
inside it?

11. two ghosts

When I say the word father - I picture him across the
dinner table.

I can see him chewing on his roughened knuckles,
choppy fingernails scratching his

                                               sun damaged skin. His
uneven stubble and a deep bruised purple
underneath his eyes.
                                                          I
focus on these small details, these things.
You know your father,
                you know who he is.

He's forty, he works for a company that sells yogurt, he
enjoys beer and cricket and ugly ties

                                                              You
know your father loves you, and he's a good man. This is
what you know, a paragraph of an introduction in your
long term memory.

This is how you make a sandwich and this is how you
add up 2 and 2

and this is the man who raised you
the one you call dad
and you're so very
sure he loves you.
How could he not? It's what he's supposed to do.
He's
supposed to wake in the morning to read the newspaper,
go to the office, and remember to love his daughter.

Dad, I need to tell you something.
When I was a child I painted a picture of our family. It
was a cheap watercolour I got gifted for my birthday,
with thin weak brushes. You stood taller than any of us,
and I wondered in the future if I could paint myself taller
than you. I couldn't draw your face very well but there
you were, a half watery giant of a man with one hand
around your wife and one around your daughter.

But as the years go by the pencil dots of your eyes blend
into the diluted peach paint.
It's been years and I've noticed that your hand doesn't
seem to be wrapped
around my shoulder at all.

So maybe it was the hope of youth,
Maybe it's the bitterness of growing up.

I want to sit across from you at our table and be
silent.   Be just like you.
I want to call you, but you're a whole life away.

When you're little your father is the world, and you are
his world.

                    Love is not such a complicated word, it just
means he reads you stories at night
                            and helps you with maths
homework.
Somewhere along the line you take a knife to yourself,
cut out skin and flesh and brains to

                                    carve a new you. So
your dad, like the brave man he is,
puts your old self in his office bag and carries it with him
for the rest of his life.
                            So now you eat dinner silently
and he doesn't care that your light is on till 2am.

You're digging through dirt
                        and mud
                            and blood in his bag,
looking for the one he loved.
You're really looking for hope.
You're looking to be saved.

                                      She didn't need it,
but you do. She was saved, whoever you were.

But you never learnt stitching from your grandmother
because it was boring, so now you're stuck with this
body, stuck with this slimy, disfigured thing, this
frankenstein that wants to fill its flesh with devotion.
No of course religion is real,

                    Of course God is real.
God is real which is why he sent you here
and which is why your dad picked you up early on
friday to get ice cream, and you hear sweet rock

                    music and laughter from the carseat.
Dad, if I asked would you come back? If I cut myself up
again, threw it all away, so you could teach me how to
build a vessel of love.
Will you paint me a new picture? Your little girl in your
arms, sketch out our smiles and eyes really
defined.   Can I stick it up on the fridge, next to the
cheap magnets of every country we've been?

I think it's only us in this lonely world.
Two ghosts circling each other.
                                      I forget you had a
part in making me,

I forget sometimes the loneliness within you is the
loneliness within me.

I want to believe in god again.
I want to believe in you again.

When I think of the word father - I see a man my height
walking around the house.
                                                    He's
looking at me like he doesn't know me.
                                        And he doesn't.
His sweet girl is dead in a body bag, and he keeps the
flies out.

            He keeps me out I mean.
I left this house a long time ago, so I hope you gave her a
burial.
I don't want to see her at your grave.
                        I don't know if you loved me, but it's
all the same. I'm turning the light out at 11, just in case
you're waiting outside the door. And if you want to
come in,

            just knock.

12. notes scratched out before sleeping

The weather's been fair recently - to me

                                       I don't
suppose I know too much about how it is for you
The little clock says it's two am for you.
                four for me.
                           I walked by Olive
Garden earlier and thought of you.

I've been seeing you kind of everywhere actually

You're in butterfly lampshades and I
        catch your shadow disappearing around the
corner.
In zip up pink jackets hung on mannequins and
              any woman with a thick kohl under
her eyes makes me hopeful for a split second
It's all useless now.
                    All this collected,
printed fact sheet about you gingerly filed in my mind
under people I love.
                I told you that once, when
we were fighting.

What do I do with my love?
                              Where does all this
information and love go?

I suppose I've always been a decent prophet, predicting
my own misfortunes.

                                    .

I barely even remembered how it happened
But I walk past you as if we
                                    haven't spilled
secrets and ripped ourselves to shreds laughing. As if the
love wasn't palpable on a dark night, I love you lilting in
the windy breeze.

It's probably for the best. Isn't that what everyone
says?   You'll forget all about it. It was my fault,
              but you weren't such a saint
either.   I miss you like a sister.
We were never much good with each other, but
sometimes we were soft.
Laid down armour and
         shields and walls.
              You never did it a lot, and I did most
often,
 it angered me beyond all means.   The next
time you left yourself defenceless I stabbed you, revenge
for the hurt I felt.

Revenge is supposed to feel sweet right? Supposed to
feel great.

                           Seeing the betrayal
and shock on your face that hardened the fact that I
would never see any kind of love in your eyes ever
again

                 cracked my entire psyche.

You didn't say it much, but I will – I love you
I'm sorry.
Stay soft.

13. the altar

I stopped believing in God on a warm February evening.
I had nothing to say, and like every bad breakup, I
walked two miles to sit on a bench and smoke.

I thought about every little argument, every time I didn't
have faith in Him, every time He let me down.
His narcissistic personality and self-serving ways, how
everyone adored Him in a way I couldn't.
          His suffocation and control, the things I
could and couldn't do,

  who I could love and couldn't love.
I took the subway home and told my mom we called it
quits.
I guess she loved Him to the point where

              all she said was
that she'd have a chat with Him about this.

So it's no more church on Sundays for me, no talking on
the floor before sleeping, no prayers before eating, no
frustration at His absence, no feeling like I've been
conned, no arguments about who I'm marrying.

Like every bad breakup, I still see Him everywhere.

In other people holding the books we once read, or a
song the choir belts as I quickly cross the street. In
celebrations I spend alone, and sometimes, when I wake
up in the middle of the night, I

                                    realize what I've done, and
sometimes, I want it back.

For the first time in ten months, I stepped foot in a
church on a cold November evening,
 headed straight for the altar.
I knelt down with my head against the wooden steps,
                                         snow
melting and running over the scarf in my lap.

I said,
Father, may someone forgive You, for You have sinned.
You have been the knife that twists and the salve on my
wound.
The gun at my temple and the guilt that gathers
underneath my skin.
Your worst crime was letting me believe I could have
been saved—no, that I needed saving.
But sometimes, when I wake up in the middle of the
night, I feel it washing all over me again.
I stay still, like I'm waiting for something to happen.

My heart beats just a little faster, and I almost see it—
almost see You.
Almost.

14. june jordan

Every autumn, this spell arises—thick layers of dust spewing around our apartment, bite marks everywhere, and coffee-stained mugs rotting in the washer. Every autumn—chewing these maple leaves, tearing up poetry books, and occasionally, a warmth in my stomach so intense I might vomit.

The clock keeps turning and turning, but I'm not sure there will ever be a moment—between twelve and eleven fifty-nine—where you want me. I was lying in wait, like a lion with its back arched on all fours, or like an injured gazelle, hoping to be taken pity upon. Either way, I was looking for relief. Maybe Death and Love feel the same— this warmth fizzing across your body until you can't breathe.

Let me do it all again, just one last time.
At least allow me to try.

Dear someone I've been loving to pass the time,
I'm happy we somehow encroached upon each other's lives. That if love was something we didn't share, loneliness and understanding were. I burned our polaroids, but only because the right way to remember

you is in my flickering memories. Besides, this apartment
—the one you're never going to see—is too small for
temporary tattoos of the past.
I'm glad we fell into each other's spring, that you loved
my June Jordan book so much I never asked for it back.
If we could keep anything of each other, I'd want us to
keep the feeling after it was all over. Like I swallowed
bittersweet jasmines along with your heart and floated
under an incalescent sun.
This was the perfect ending to everything. And I hope
you know—I wouldn't have changed it, even if I could
have. If that means anything to you.
I hope it does.

15. an instructional manual on feeling loveable

You can't be miserable / That's the first thing / Get off your bed / Don't stare at the ceiling / Don't look at the artificial light / Don't roll over and let your legs go weak and think about a girl you gave / your all to / Wash your face / Open the window / Pull the strings of memories out / (the friends who left) / Take that box of trinkets and wash it down the drain / (the things they left) / you can't let yourself be / the thing left behind / Please don't stare at your reflection / Cover the mirror with the old blanket in your brother's room that nobody uses / Stop holding the phone up to search for her name / You're ignoring all your friends / Throw the phone across your bed / Read a good book, strong vigorous chapters / Should feel like you're chopping wood / and you're good at it / Have a sliced pear and sit on the kitchen counter / Let the soft evening sun hold your back / I know you wish it was her / But it never was / Your loneliness is a projector / You're standing behind the camera / hands trembling / But she had to leave the screen eventually / he had to leave the screen eventually / How long can a movie go on / You're running out of film / You're also running out of cereal / Go outside and go to the farther supermarket / Buy some flowers and / cut the stems off them / Don't look too hard at the fast cars and their / reckless drivers / Stop imagining / Eat a biscuit or even have two / The dull ache in your heart / I know it's crying out / Get on your knees / Sing about something / sing about god / Call your friends / They don't hate you / Hug a tree really tightly / Don't pretend like it's her / Inhale in with a sharp breath the dead leaves / baby leaves / Your grief is trying to drown you / Kick your legs up and float / Listen to the chatter in the distance / Think about the train you're taking home / They're all moving, jostling, thinking / A life of moving and / moving and / moving / When you slip into bed / don't let the salt reach your ears / You were always enough / Unlock your door / Let love slip into the bed beside you / It's been with you the whole day / Let it tuck your hair behind your ears, even if / you only feel your own touch / Turn out the light / Dream of the train tomorrow / You are so loved

16. one man cult

Every week, we gather and dream about you. Candle
wax melts on my wrists, and I'm praying to you to stop
the pain. I know I will endure any pain for you.
I read your words every night. I have to close my eyes
and exhale—I feel you wherever I am. For every sin
uttered, I am met with something worth more than
forgiveness—a laugh. The fervor rushes through me and
levitates my entire body. I need nobody's proof that you
are holy.
I will resurrect the Romans, and they will tear down
their churches and stain all the windows with the amber
of your eyes. My hands quiver in your presence, and my
stomach feels sick with devotion. I do not care who I was
born to or who will be born to me—as far as I know, the
entire point was you.
I can't even look at you. The Greeks said that if they
looked at their gods in pure form, they would eviscerate
—and they were right. Every molecule of skin, flesh, and
eye formulated aeons ago exists to consume you.
Right at the top of my throat, at the underside of my
mouth, lie all the words I want to tell you. But if they
ever crawled up, they would be a soft scream followed by
endless sobbing. I am worried that if I touch you, I will
taint you.

To paint you or write about you feels like a disservice, an injustice of the worst kind. The only way to worship and understand you is to be with you—to close my eyes and feel the religion capsizing my body, to know I am a part of something bigger than myself.

17. revelations

I look at your hands through the crack of bathroom light, spilling over a fraction of you.
Your hands have been soft since birth / covered in blood since birth.
I see the ridges and evanescent outlines running through —roots of where you came from.
The sloppy clipping and lopsided shape of your nails—a testament to your mother's carelessness. I linger in the bathroom doorway and think about your hands that have seen your life, borne the weight of mine, and stayed soft.
When I slip into bed, you don't even wake up to put your arm right under my ribcage. I lie still in the pitch black and feel as though I've swallowed a hundred stars, glittering with hope and shine in this cramped, big-city apartment.
So much of loving you has been a quiet revelation. A rebirth, almost—I can feel enlightenment whispering in my ears. No life is without you, or death. For all the times I've drawn blood and snarled at you like a dog. Sometimes, I'm still a stray, wondering why I got taken in. The guilt sits in my chest and grows heavier every day.
I am yours in the sweetest way possible. I am yours, like

the rings of stain on a coffee cup, like blurred letters in a newspaper against damp fingers, like the dent in a heavily used armchair. An imprint that just happened— simply the effect of existing around each other. Memories of our love are etched into everything we touch. Irretrievably, we are changing each other every second.

18. my final act of love

Is to keep remembering you.

Not as a ghost haunting my weeping figure, or as a
looming shadow of pain I cannot let go of,
I'll remember you as a sunny day. I'll remember you as
the first tentative bloom of spring. How good a warm
home can feel after a cold day. Over and over I will
remember these snippets, these snapshots, and think
about how lucky I was to feel for someone this way. To
know how big my heart can swell, how deep my love
goes. Over time, how the acceptance weaved itself into
whatever tattered pieces of love (I think they call it grief)
I had left.
My final act of love — is allowing you to keep whatever
love I had for you. It's yours now. I don't want it back,
because I regret nothing now. I feel like I'm breathing
properly for the first time since 13.

Sometimes grief is letting go
Acknowledging its real name - love
Sometimes it's just time moving forward
Light streaming through the kitchen

19. these violent delights

I have seen this scene.
On movie, replaying
       Replaying in my mind.
              Replaying in daydreams and
nightmares
                        and perhaps
dreams more unbefitting to tell

              It's the same.
You're drinking like you've locked away a spare liver.
                    I'm there with a
boy you don't care about and you're there with girls I
want to strangle.
       Your eyes glint like gold.

                  I know / I
know it's a farce, I'm the only one who knows. You
vampires with your promises of love fulfilled.

          your stare burns on my face. A
violent heat incinerates the blush.

Oh your eyes / eyes of sin,

                              I imagine this was how it
felt for Lucifer
                                                  God's
most beautiful, tumbling down from heaven. Eyes of
desire, eyes of want, of hunger, of need.

I can feel the yearning glowering on you, it looks almost
tender
                          a haze of white enveloping
us.   You are no angel, that much I know.

It's as though a gun has been pressed up against my
head, an acute ache spreading through the fog.
                    Your fangs sink into my flesh, crimson
streams run down my collarbones

I have promised you blood, truthfully it is I gaining.
                                        At least the blood
seeping into you is mine / at least you are mine.

I muse about you cutting me open with a butter-knife,
chewing on bits of me.
              Flesh melting in your mouth.
                                  Nerves and sinew and blood all
a part of you.
                                                  No
longer mine, together in the truest sense.

A kind of closeness most can dream about.

 I wonder if you're thinking of mangling
me,   ripping me apart with teeth and hands,
                              devouring me not in
wickedness, but in religion

It's not barbarism, no it's not that simple,
                              didn't Jesus
offer his flesh and blood for his disciples? Why should
this be any different?

*Are you thinking of dismembering me? Of bringing my
heart into your heart?*

An invisible resolve tightens, it's a lot more calm.
                    Do it, eat me alive, make us one,
take my heart

Your canines pierce my skin.

20. point of no return

The shortest poem I have written is about love.

Nothing much to say except for your name, the warmth of the sun and an inexplicable joy to be alive, thrumming through these streets. I'm watching this beautiful light take possession of my life. I think about us eating well, perhaps a steaming tomato soup. Putting on a new record.

I dream, I dream, I dream — of having nothing to say, these feelings bursting up in me over and over. Lying in summer grass and nodding to myself — it's finally the way it's supposed to be.

21. swan song

So this is how it is,
Drinking sweet iced tea in long-drawn-out June
The click shuffle of an east coast swing on wooden floors
More dishes to clean, more hot sun burning our skin
Reading with our legs kicked so far up the car seat—the
interpretation of dreams
Big, uneven smiles all over my county.

You had asked for redemption and forgiveness. Most of
all, you had asked for love.
And now we chew toffee in church / chase each other
around in our garden
The sweet voices of the Temptations drifting through the
kitchen
While I braid your hair

Tomorrow we're driving out for no good reason at all
Whatever we do these days seems to be for no good
reason at all
But you once told me we don't need to have one. Who
cares?
I'm staring out the car window on a Tuesday dawn

Here comes the life you've always wanted
Here comes the beautiful, rising sun.